Praying the Prayers of the Apostle Paul

Discovering the **Power** of **Prayer** in Your Life

Chris Sparkman

Strategic Book Publishing
New York, New York

Strategic Book Publishing
An imprint of AEG Publishing Group
845 Third Avenue, 6th Floor—6016
New York, NY 10022
http://www.strategicbookpublishing.com

ISBN: 978-1-60693-881-2, 1-60693-881-9

Book Design: Bruce Salender

Printed in the United States of America

Dedication

To my wife Sherri. I am so blessed to have you in my life. Thank you for sticking by me all these years and supporting my dreams. You are an awesome woman, wife, and mom. I love you.

Contents

Introduction

I have always heard pastors and Bible teachers comment on the need for Christians to spend time with God in prayer. They told of how prayer can make a difference and how prayer was, in effect, communication with God. So, like most Christians, I prayed. Not as diligently as I should, but I still put in my time talking to God.

Then, as my life changed, I was challenged to experience more of what God had for my life, for my family, and for my church. I realized that if I was going to experience something different, something powerful, then something was missing. I talked with leaders and observed those who were really doing something powerful for the Kingdom, and I realized what these people had in common—they all spent time alone with God. Not the kind of time I was spending with God, but meaningful, quality, time.

My prayer partner, and what I like to call prayer mentor, challenged me to look into the prayer life of the Apostle Paul and see what I could learn. From that challenge arose what you will read in the forthcoming pages. I realized that if my prayer life was going to lead to God's power being evidenced in my life, there were specifics that needed to be included in my prayer time, and there were lifestyle changes that needed to be made. Many of these changes could only be brought about through prayer.

It is my desire that, as you read through the pages of this book, you will be challenged to pray more, and that you will be challenged to change the way you pray and get specific when you approach God. It is my hope that your life will change through your prayers. It is my prayer that you, like me, will begin to experience the power of God in your life on a daily basis—the power of God that will open the doors for you to become all that God has intended for your life and for His Kingdom.

Chapter 1
Prayer and the Believer

For the believer, prayer is a vehicle used to communicate with God. Through prayer, we also find an unlimited source of power that is associated with spending time in communion with God. Through our times of communion with God, we discover that it is possible for the child of God to see this power manifested in their own life, as well as in the lives of those who they pray with and pray for.

Through prayer, we see a power that is able to change the world in which we live. I not only speak of the things that we desire to see accomplished in our own lives, such as healing, financial freedom, broken relationships restored, and renewed communion with the Father; I am also saying that prayer brings with it the power to impact those surrounding us. Prayer can change your situation at work, it can lead your church to grow, and it can cause those without Christ to desire the light they see in you. Prayer can lead your spouse to love and appreciate you more, it can cause your children to make the right decisions, and prayer can even make you a better dad or mom and husband or wife.

Through prayer, we see a power revealing itself through an intimate relationship with God. The Bible clearly teaches us that when we draw near to God, that God draws near to us (Ps. 145:18). The great news surrounding this is that the closer you desire to walk with God, the closer God walks with you. This intimate relationship allows you to know more about God, and when you see yourself in the light of His character, you will humble yourself all the more by seeking to become more like Him. What this does for the believer is that it leads him or her to a life of holiness and obedience. We know from Scripture that God desires obedience, and that obedience leads to power and blessing.

Through prayer, we discover the power that is found within us through the indwelling of the Holy Spirit. There are some important issues to accept and embrace when considering the indwelling of the Spirit. First, this indwelling takes place the moment salvation is received. When we enter into a personal relationship with Jesus Christ, the Holy Spirit comes into our hearts to take up a personal residence. What this means is that a member of the Godhead is living inside of you! It gets even better. This indwelling of the Holy Spirit is a permanent feature. The Bible clearly teaches us that when the Spirit comes into our hearts, it seals us unto the day of redemption. Remember this important truth about God: He does not make mistakes! Once He gives you a gift, He will not repent of that gift by removing the blessing from your life, and this includes the presence of the Holy Spirit.

With the Holy Spirit dwelling in our lives, we are taught by the author of Hebrews that we can then boldly approach the throne of Grace (Heb. 4:16). This verse is not teaching us to approach God with a flippant attitude, giving very little thought to what is being said. It reveals to us the power of coming to God with reverence because He is the King and Lord of your life, and further, coming to Him with a bold assurance that He will not only hear, but also answer, because He is your Friend and Counselor.

In consideration of the power that has been placed literally at the threshing floor of your heart, what are some practical ways that we can release this power in our lives and experience the continuous presence of the Spirit?

I believe the answer to this question is found as you and I begin praying the will of God. I know the confusion that sometimes surrounds this statement. After all, what is the will of God? I am not necessarily speaking to the specific will that God has for your life, but the will of God as communicated to us through the Scripture.

What do we know about God's will? We understand that it is His will for souls to be saved. Jesus tells us in the Gospel of Luke that it is not God's will for any to perish, but for all to come to repentance. It is His will for the church to grow. Nowhere in Scripture, will you find it acceptable for the church to plateau or decrease in size. In every reference to the church, we see that men and women are being added daily, such as should be saved. Let me remind you that the church is a living organism, and thus it should be in a perpetual state of growth. It is His will for the believer to experience life, but not merely life, life more abundant and free. God desires for His children to be free from the bondage of their sin and their former lives. He desires us to be free to serve His Son and to live in the liberties that come through this personal relationship. God desires for us to enjoy our walk with Him and to be ourselves, not a made up caricature of what "religion" has told us to be. Finally, it is His will for the life of the believer to bear fruit upon the earth. Not only bearing fruit by reproducing other believers, but the fruit of the Spirit being evidenced in our life, which Paul describes for us in Gal. 5:22 when he says, "But when the Holy Spirit controls our lives, he will produce this kind of fruit in us: love, joy, peace, patience, kindness, goodness, faithfulness, gentleness, and self-control. Here there is not conflict with the law." (New Living Translation)

I would also say that anytime you are praying any type of Kingdom or Calling prayer, you can know that you are on solid ground with the will of God. Since this terminology may be new to you, let me explain in further detail.

Kingdom prayers are prayers that are offered to God with the intent of seeing the Kingdom of God advanced upon the earth. There are no ulterior motives, no self-promotion, just God's Kingdom being increased.

Calling prayers are prayers that reflect your calling. You are called, right? Therefore, what you should be seeking in life is to fulfill God's call for you. Your calling should be sure. You should be able to say, "This is what God has called me to do." Understand, calling prayers very seldom end with, "if it be thy will." The reason for this is simple, if you believe that God has placed a call upon your life, to pray any other way would be to doubt God's call. Consider the requests made by Paul in Eph. 6 and Col. 4. In both cases, Paul is in prison. When he communes with God, he does not pray for deliverance from prison, instead he asks the churches to pray for open doors to share the Gospel and for boldness to speak and a clarity to receive. Why does Paul pray this way? He understands what he is called to do!

If you seek to unleash the power of God upon your life through your prayer time, I also encourage you to begin to be more specific in the ways that you pray and in the things that you ask God to do. We must find a way to approach God with the right attitude and motive, and many times this is found in the way you ask God to do something.

Let me illustrate it for you in the following way. What do you say when asked if you want something to eat? Most often we will say, "Whatever you have," and this leaves the door wide-open for you to receive anything, even something that you do not want. However, when asked the same question, if you say, "I would like a hamburger, fries, and a large vanilla milkshake," then you have been specific, and therefore your host knows what to bring you. This is what I believe God desires through our prayers. He wants us to be specific. He wants us to share with Him what is on our heart and what it is we need Him to do. When you pray in this way, you will release the power of God through your prayers.

Chapter 2
Paul's Prayer Life

When we come together to consider the prayer life of the Apostle Paul, we learn some very valuable lessons on the importance of prayer and how to use prayer as an avenue to God. I believe from the very beginning, Paul truly believed that there was power in prayer. From the outset of his ministry, Paul shows us that when he had a need, he took that need to God in prayer. We see Paul praying for provision, deliverance, freedom, boldness, salvation, and healing throughout the book of Acts and in the Epistles. Why would a man pray so much about so many different things? The only obvious conclusion is that Paul believed God answered prayer.

Let me ask you a very timely question: Do you believe that God answers prayer? Additionally, let me give you something a little deeper to consider. Do you believe that God answers *your* prayers? There is a difference, and I believe that the answer to this question made a difference in the prayer life of the Apostle Paul. I also believe it makes a difference in our prayer lives as well.

If you believe that God answers prayer, you are right, He does. However, this knowledge alone will not cause you to habitually spend time in prayer. This knowledge will lead you to pray on occasion. This knowledge will lead you to prayer when crisis comes to your life or to your family. This knowledge will allow you to see God to some good things, yet it will hinder you from seeing God do great things. The person who simply believes God answers prayer is typically a person who does not spend much time in prayer. This person is also atypical of those who rely on the prayers of others for their help and strength, rather than going to God to receive from Him themselves.

Drawing from this, if you believe God answers your prayer, then you are right, He does! Possessing the knowledge that God not only hears you when you pray, but He also steps in to intervene by answering your prayers, unlocks a huge amount of potential. What this means for you is that you now have the ability to partner with God to change things! This is what we see happening throughout the Bible as men and women sought God, and as these same men and women saw God step in and literally change the outcome of their situation. When you believe that God answers your prayers, you will begin to pray. When you pray, things begin to happen. The Apostle Paul not only believed that God answered prayer; he believed that God answered his prayers, and he prayed.

The next lesson we gain from observing the prayer life of Paul is that he was persistent in the things that he prayed. Time and time again, we read in the Scriptures that Paul continually went before the Lord on behalf of others. We read that he always thanked God for the believers and their churches (1 Cor. 1:4), constantly mentioning them in his prayers (Rom. 1:9). In every prayer, he prays with joy for them (Phil. 1:4), and asks that he constantly remember them in his prayers (1 Thess. 5:17). Even in his own words, Paul tells us to be persistent in prayer (Rom. 12:12).

It seems as if Paul knew the secret that we often forget in our prayer life—if you keep asking, it will be given to you. If you keep searching, you will find. If you keep knocking, the door will be opened to you (Matt. 7:7–8). What the Master

Teacher is telling us in this Scripture is the same thing the Apostle Paul is saying and modeling; be persistent in your prayer life.

I can relate with what some of you may be thinking right about now. You have asked, sought, and knocked, and you still have not received or found, and no door has been opened. During dry spells such as these, it is easy for us to simply quit being persistent. It is not that we have lost faith, or even that we doubt God's ability to grant. Most of the time, we quit asking due to the belief that if God does not grant some request right away, it must not be His will. Should this be said? Do not sell God short of what He wants to accomplish in your life. If you believe in your heart that God has something more for you, keep asking, seeking, and knocking. Remember, with the belief that God answers your prayers, you have the ability to change your life with God.

When we consider the prayer life of Paul, we also note that Paul was not ashamed to ask others to pray for him. He was open in asking the churches to pray for others, and it seems as if there were no limits to the things that Paul would request in prayer. On one occasion, Paul asks the Rom. if they would agonize with him in prayer that he would be delivered from the unbelievers in Judea. He wanted his service in Jerusalem to be acceptable to the saints, and that it would be God's will for him to come to Rome (Rom. 15:30). What Paul is doing is similar to what Jesus does with His disciples; Paul is inviting the church to join in his struggles by means of prayer.

Prayer becomes a weapon in the arsenal of believers as we intercede for others who join with us in our fight against Satan. In Ephesians 6, Paul lists for us the weapons that we, as believers, are to use during our warfare with the evil one. Paul tells those who read this epistle that with every prayer, they are to pray at all times in the Spirit. They are to stay alert and persevere in intercession for all the saints. When Paul asks us to pray for all the saints, he is asking us to pray for all believers in Christ, those whom you know, and those whom you have never met, that are fighting the good fight of the faith all around this world.

We stress the importance of being partners in ministry. We strive to find ways to get our people and our churches working together to further the Kingdom here on earth. If we model our lives after the life of the Apostle Paul, could it be that the greatest partnership we can have while living on this earth is to agree and partner with one another in prayer? What would happen if churches began to pray for one another? What would happen if individual Christians were moved to spend time praying for one another, not just when facing a crisis, but praying for strength and wisdom and the ability to be used as part of God's will? I have an idea of what the results might look like. More power for the individual and the church to live for Christ. More love for the church and the individual to share with a world that desperately needs to experience the love of Christ. Finally, an indwelling presence of the Holy Spirit of God that would lead us, both as individuals and churches, into the fullness of all things promised through the Word of God. Learn from Paul and do not be hesitant to request prayer for yourself, others, and for the movement of God in your life.

Next, it seems as if the prayers of the Apostle Paul seem to follow a pattern, yet, at the same time, they were specific to each congregation or person that he was praying for. When we look closer at the way Paul prays, he usually begins by thanking God for the person or church, and the work that God is doing in their life or ministry. He prays that they will grow in the knowledge of Jesus Christ, and that they will be able to differentiate between what is right and wrong, good and bad, vital and trivial. He then addresses a congregation's individual needs.

Let me offer a few examples. For the Romans, Paul prays that he will be allowed to visit them and preach the Gospel unto them (Rom. 1:10). For the Corinthian church, Paul prays that they will do no wrong and that they will pass the test and be found faithful (2 Cor. 13:7). For those at Ephesus and abroad, he prays that the eyes of their hearts may be enlightened (Eph. 1:18). For the Phil., he prays them to be filled with the fruit of righteousness (Phil. 1:11). He prays that the Colossian believers would stay devoted to prayer and to thanksgiving (Col. 4:2). To the believers at Thessalonica, that God would cause them to increase and overflow with love toward each other and everyone, and that God would consider them worthy of His calling and, by His power, fulfill every desire for goodness and the work of faith (1 Thess. 3:12 and 2 Thess. 1:11). So even though each prayer includes the same basic components, they call become specific to the congregation.

How does this apply to you, me, and our prayer life? Easy. When we find ourselves in a time of prayer, we must remember that the same prayers do not apply everywhere we go. If we are going to experience the power of God through prayer, we must specifically pray to each circumstance in which we find ourselves encompassed. When we pray that God will bless a congregation, we need to ask, how does God need to bless them? Then, pray specifically for that blessing. When you pray that God heal an individual, be specific and pray about what God needs to do. Paul understood this concept, and although many of his prayers included the same basic components, he tailored each prayer to meet the need of those he was praying for. We should do the same.

We also discover through Paul that he was genuinely concerned for those he prayed for and the work in which they were doing for the Kingdom. One of the amazing things I discovered through the study of the Apostle Paul's prayer life is the tremendous memory that he must have possessed, for he always makes mention of the needs of the churches and people he has ministered to when he went to the Lord in prayer. Now, given Paul's network of influence, he must have spent a great deal of time before the Lord, and from his tone, I do not think this time was laborious to him, but a joy.

When you truly care for someone, you will pray for them. Far too many times, we tell those with whom we come in contact with that we will pray for them, and then never do. The sad thing about this statement is that many times these people are counting on you to take their need before the throne of grace for them and with them. At other times when we do pray for others, we approach God with a tone that communicates we are tired or that it is a chore for us to spend our time in prayer on someone else rather than ourselves. If we are going to experience God's power through our prayer life, we have to come to the place where we are ready to put the needs of other's before our own needs. We will have to come to the place where we do not dread lifting up the needs and burdens of others, but we actually see it as joy to be counted worthy to petition our heavenly Father on their behalf and for His glory. Paul discovered this in his prayer life, and therefore Paul spent much time praying for the needs of those he cared for.

Finally, when praying, Paul always found a reason to offer up thanks for those he prayed for. A closer look will show that, even though Paul was addressing serious problems within the local church, and at times doctrinal errors, he was thankful for his fellow brothers and sisters in Christ. Paul was found thanking God for the grace they had received, for the witness of the church throughout the world, for their spirit of wisdom and Rev., and for the fact that when they heard the word, they received the word.

There is power in thanking God for what he is doing in the world and what he is doing in the lives of those around you. That is exactly what this book is about. Understanding how to pray prayers of thanksgiving for what God is doing in the life of His church and in individual believers. If you can learn to approach prayer with an attitude of thanksgiving, you will unlock a new level of spiritual power that can only come from God.

I invite you to join me on our journey through the prayers of thanks offered by the Apostle Paul.

Chapter 3
Praying for Others

First, I thank my God through Jesus Christ for you all, because your faith is being proclaimed throughout the whole world. (Rom. 1:8) (New American Standard Bible)

Paul begins the Epistle to the church at Rome by saying he thanks God for them and for the witness of their faith that has spread around the world. This is an amazing statement in itself when we consider the environment that the Roman Christians were exposed to during the first century. If you recall, Rome was the western world's political center at this time; which would mean that it was neither an area conducive to the Christian life, nor would it have been a very desirable atmosphere for a Christian to live in. The majority of church members would have been Gentile believers who were highly visible in the world. The good news for this church, as Paul expresses to us, is their reputation was excellent. Their level of faith, which was very strong, was making its way around the known world, and Paul says that, for this, he is thankful.

The faith of this church really is incredible when we consider that soon, in AD 70, because of their faith, Nero would crucify some one-thousand believers by setting them on fire—the same faith that Paul is commending them for.

It would do us good to remember that even though Paul would eventually lose his life in Rome for the cause of Christ, it is unlikely that he actually founded this church. The church in Rome was probably founded by one of two sources: it may have been founded by those converted during the events of Pentecost (Acts 2:10), or it may have been founded by a convert of Paul or one of the other apostles who carried back the Word of God and started a church there to reach the Gentiles.

One thing we do know for certain, Paul was a missionary and a church planter, and his prayer life should serve as an example to us, as individuals, and to the church today. I would like you to consider that the Apostle Paul was not envious, jealous, or bitter about the work that was taking place in Rome. He did not try to overshadow the work that was taking place by promoting his own calling or agenda. Instead, Paul praised God for what the believers in the church at Rome were doing. Paul took the opportunity to encourage them and to share insights into the Scriptures that would strengthen them. Paul even expressed his desire to be with them so that he could share in what God was doing in and through the church.

We need to foster a greater desire to follow Paul's pattern today. The church today needs to understand that we are growing the Kingdom of God and that we are not in competition with those churches and ministries that surround our own. It is time for us to understand that a soul, saved, is a soul, saved, whether that happens through our work or someone else's work. Then, when we see or hear about that soul being saved, we need to rejoice with them and for them. We must begin to see that it is growth of the Kingdom growth, not "my" church growth. We must come to the point where we stop seeing other Bible-believing, Bible-teaching, and Bible-preaching churches as a threat or hindrance to our own ministries, and see them instead as a resource to join with to do something great for the Kingdom of God.

Through looking at Paul's prayer that he directed towards the church at Rome, I believe he is teaching us that when we go before the Father in prayer, we should take the time to praise God for churches that are a part of our denominations, as well as for those who are not. We need to begin to thank God for the work and the faith that is evidenced all around us through these different ministries.

Following are a few things that I believe we can begin to thank God for when we see or hear of other ministries or churches. We can thank God for the vision that He has placed within the hearts of the leaders and members of each congregation or ministry. Different churches are doing different things, yet they are all working towards the same goal—the growth of the Kingdom. Along these same lines, we need to thank God for the ministries that are offered at each church. Here is the sticky part for many, instead of being thankful that the church down the road that has a deaf ministry, some become envious and think that their church needs this ministry or that their church could do a better job at that ministry. The truth is, God gave the other church that vision, and you need to thank God for the vision that He gave to them and spend more time seeking His vision for your own church. Churches and ministries are full of people with differing gifts; therefore, I do not believe we were all meant to be doing the same thing. Furthermore, people enjoy different things, and if all churches or ministries offered the same thing, where would the people seeking something different go? We need to thank God for the vision of the differing ministries we see around us. We need to thank God for the things that others have that we do not, and at the same time, thank Him for those things that we have in common that the other ministry may do better than we do.

We also should be thanking God for the gifted believers that He has placed in each position of leadership to serve and worship in a church or through a ministry. I like to see the name of the pastor outside on a church sign, that way I can not only pray for the church when I am driving by, but I can pray for that pastor specifically and thank God that he is being obedient to the call that God has placed on his life. When we pass by a ministry building or church and we know someone who worships or leads there, we should thank God for them and the job they are doing, even if they are doing a better job than we are. Remember, the key is being thankful!

We should also thank God when we hear of Biblical church growth taking place. What is Biblical church growth? Well, first it is not transferring disgruntled church members from one side of town to the other. I remember a time that I mentioned to a group of pastors the need to stop all of the transferring of membership that was happening between our group of churches. One pastor stepped up and said that if we continued this, he wouldn't have any church growth to show for the year. Friends, that is not growing a church Biblically. If you want to thank God for something, thank God for a church that is growing due to men and women coming to know Christ as their Savior. Thank God for churches that are going out into the highways and byways, finding those who are unchurched or who have become disenchanted with the church and bringing them in, and bringing them home, to the Father. I believe that two things should take place within our hearts when we hear that a church is growing Biblically, 1) we should immediately thank God for that church, and 2) it should inspire us to see our church grow through reaching the lost and unchurched for Christ as well.

We should thank God when we see churches adding buildings for ministry. More ministries mean more souls saved, which means Kingdom growth, and for that we should be thankful. Remember our example, Paul, he was not envious, jealous, or bitter about what was happening in Rome. Instead, he was thankful, and he even desired to be with them so that he could rejoice in what God was doing. We need to follow this pattern and rejoice that God is doing something good in other ministries, and then if you are led, pray that God will do something where you worship and serve. All it takes is one person getting on fire for God for this flame to spread to other people, then fueling their faith for greatness.

Finally, we need to thank the Lord when we see or hear of new churches that are being planted. **A Church plant occurs when a Church is started, from scratch, out of a desire to reach a community that is not yet being reached by an existing church.** Church planting is a Biblical way to grow a church. I understand the concern that most churches are not full, so why do we need another church. Statistics show that people will begin attending a new church faster than they will a church that is already established. I think for most people, we like the idea of having a fresh start. A new church plant gives these people a fresh start. Therefore, we need to avoid the trap of complaining that the new church is not like all the other churches in town. We need to stop worrying about "our" territory being violated and begin rejoicing and thanking God that a new church has come to the area, and that Kingdom growth is about to take place.

I want to state clearly that I believe Paul's ministry was successful, and his prayer life powerful, because he learned how to appreciate and give thanks to God for the Kingdom work that was going on around him. If you desire more success and power in your ministry and prayer life, it would do you well to learn how to give thanks also.

Here are some thought provoking questions for you to consider:

- What believers do you know that are currently growing in their faith?
- What Churches do you know that are currently growing either spiritually, numerically, or both?
- What ministries do you see God using?
- What churches do you know that are involved in church planting?
- Do you know any church planters?

- Have you seen churches doing things, or becoming something, that you wish your church would do or become?

After considering your answers, pray that God will release you from any feelings of envy or bitterness towards another church, ministry, or Christian. Once you feel the peace that only comes from God filling your heart, pray that God will allow you to see others not as a threat to your ministry or church, but as partners in the work of God. Here is the final step to applying this first example of Paul to your prayer life: begin right now to offer up thanks for what you see going on around you for the sake of the Kingdom. Allow this practice to become habit for you. When you hear what others are doing, when you think about another ministry, and even as you drive down the road, may you always find yourself thanking God for His work.

I firmly believe that when we come to the place where we can genuinely pray like the Apostle Paul, we will work together and not against one another. When we get to this place, we truly see the power of God released upon our lives as we see answers to prayer, and we are made more useful to the Kingdom as we experience both spiritual and numerical growth.

Chapter 4
Praying for Grace

I thank my God always concerning you for the grace of God which was given you in Christ Jesus.... (1 Cor. 1:4)

The prayer life of the Apostle Paul was powerful because he actually believed in the God who answers prayer, and he was persistent in his prayer life. When Paul prayed, he was specific to the needs of the individual or the congregation, and he showed genuine care and concern for all those he prayed for and for the work that they were carrying forth for the good of the Kingdom. There also appears to be a righteous element and a will of God element in Paul's prayer life. Paul sought to live a life that was in the will of God, while at the same time wanting the will of God above his own will. He allowed these elements to guide him as he prayed.

In the previous chapter, we discussed how one thing, specifically, opened up the effectiveness of Paul's prayer life— and that was his own willingness to give thanks for the work that was going on around him. Although Paul was not directly involved with the church at Rome, he thanked God for what the believers in Rome were doing under the threat of persecution and death. The reason Paul was able to do this is that he realized what was going on was far bigger than him; it was about the Kingdom of God.

As you contemplate the points shared throughout this book about opening up to the power of God in your life and ministry by using the example of the Apostle Paul in your prayer life, you must learn to focus more of your time with God and be thankful for what God is doing in your life and in the lives of other believers. Doing so will, undoubtedly, give you access to the same world changing power Paul had access to.

We glean our next example from Paul through his prayer for the believers in Corinth. This prayer will actually cover the next three chapters as it is full of dynamic information. It is important for us to understand Paul's prayer at this time in context to the believers he was praying for. The city of Corinth was a port city and a very wealthy commercial center of the day. The city housed an outdoor theater capable of seating twenty-thousand people, and hosted a series of athletic games that was second only to the Olympics, which were held in Greece. The population of the city itself was comprised of a mixture of Greek, Roman, and Asian cultures.

Corinth was also home to the great temple of Aphrodite, which housed some one-thousand temple prostitutes. To say the least, the city of Corinth was an immoral cesspool. There were taverns, located throughout the city, which came to be known for everything sinful. The term, "to act Corinthian," means to practice fornication.

Paul came to Corinth with the gospel of Jesus Christ sometime during his second missionary journey around AD 50, establishing a following, which led to a church body. While in Corinth, it appears that Paul lived and worked with Aquila and Priscilla, and shared his message throughout the synagogues. As was custom for Paul, opposition forced him out of the synagogue, and he began preaching from home of Titius Justus.

Paul continued here with the church for roughly eighteen months.

After Paul had departed, word came to him about the condition of the church, which motivated him to write the letter to the Corinthians in order to answer several questions the people had concerning divisions in the church (Cor. 1:11), immorality (Cor. 5 and 6:9–20), along with marriage, food, worship, and the resurrection. Despite where the believers found themselves and the conditions surrounding the city and the church, Paul found several reasons to praise God for the believers and the church in Corinth.

> I thank my God always concerning you for the grace of God which as given you in Christ Jesus, that in everything you were enriched in Him, in all speech and all knowledge, even as the testimony concerning Christ was confirmed in you.... (1 Cor. 1:4–6)

Notice that Paul thanks God for the grace that they had received. He thanks God that they were made rich in everything, especially in speech and knowledge. Finally, he thanks God that the testimony of Christ was confirmed among them.

We will begin by considering what it meant when Paul thanked God for the grace that they had received. This, by the way, is speaking of the same grace that we saw Paul thank God for being found in the life of the Roman church in Rom. 1:8. We believe, of course, that this is speaking of the grace that was shown unto them which allowed them to become children of God.

The word *grace* is interesting when you consider the different meanings that flow from this word: 1) bestowing pleasure, or delight, or favor upon someone, 2) the power of equipment for ministry, and 3) the freeness and universality of salvation and the pleasure and joy God designs for its recipients.

28

Here, Paul is thanking God specifically for the grace that is given in Christ Jesus. The Corinthian believers were called to be saints (1 Cor. 1:2). This means that they were set apart, that they were being sanctified. This is true of the believers here because of their position in Christ. It was even true in spite of their blatant imperfections. The great news today is that the New Testament designates all believers as saints! By position, we are all holy, and by position, we have all been set apart to God (Rom. 1:7).

> Christ has saved us, and called us with a holy calling, not according to works, but according to his own purpose and grace, which was given us in Christ Jesus before the world began.... (2 Tim. 1:9)

Watch what Paul is doing here: he is affirming their privilege of belonging to the Lord and receiving this grace. Why is this important? Remember, Paul knew their current condition and he knew their mindset and how many of them were living. Thus, he was attempting to confirm them by assuring them that they still belonged to God. Many times, we run into people who have drifted or whose mindset has come under attack, and instead of spending time affirming them, we spend our time rebuking them. As a result, when they leave our presence they feel worse than when they came to us for help.

In this situation, we really need to consider what is more beneficial for this person: pointing out the fact of their sin, or moving beyond their sin and showing them that they still belong to God. I believe this is what the Apostle Paul did in his prayer, and I believe he did this because this is what Jesus does. Do you remember when Peter denied Jesus? Do you remember what Jesus said to Peter? He did not condemn him, did he? No, Jesus simply passed on a message that Peter was supposed to join the other disciples in the upper room. What was Jesus doing was affirming that Peter still belonged to God;

the same thing Paul did, and the same thing you and I should be doing as well.

By thanking God for them, he is also affirming the call that God has placed upon their lives, and reaffirming that they have a purpose for the Kingdom of God. Praise God that He can still use people who have messed up in life! If He couldn't, there wouldn't be any ministry going on at all. There are some things that would benefit us all to understand about the call of God.

First, He has called us with a holy calling.

> For God has not called us unto uncleanness, but unto holiness. (1 Thess. 4:7) (KJV)

> Therefore, Holy Brethren, partakers of a heavenly calling…. (Heb. 3:1) (NASB)

This means that God has called us to be holy, or to be set apart from this world, and set apart to serve Him. God has not called us to live impure lives. If God called you into this life of holiness, then surely He has empowered you to live holy. This empowering comes directly from the Holy Spirit living within every believer. If we will listen to His lead, and be obedient to His commands, we will be found holy.

Second, we are called according to His purpose.

> And we know that all things work together for good to them that love God, to them who are called according to His purpose. (Rom. 8:28) (NASB)

One thing which needs to be stressed, it is God's call. He is the one who issued our call to salvation. Now, he is able to use every circumstance that we encounter in this life for good. How is this possible, you may be wondering? Easy, when the Holy Spirit convinces a person to receive Christ, we are given a new outlook on life. We leave off trusting earthly treasures for our security, and begin to trust God. Trusting God allows us to know that He is with us whatever pain or persecution we may experience in this life.

Finally, we were called before the world began.

Rom. 16:25—We are called for the revelation of the mystery from before the world began.
Eph. 1:4—He has chosen us from before the foundation of the world.
Eph. 3:11—Called according to the eternal purpose
Titus 1:2—God, which cannot lie promised eternal life from before the world began.
1 Pet. 1:20—Jesus was foreordained before the foundation of the world.

God knew you, called you, and ordained you for His purpose from before the world began. I will admit that I do not understand such a wonderful truth. I will agree that it does something to our overall idea of free will. I do think, however, that this is one of the truths, which, instead of trying to rationalize, would benefit us just to accept as a blessing. He has always known you with a plan and a purpose!

Here is Paul's powerful message in this prayer. Corinthian church—you have been chosen by God, and you have been empowered to do the work of the ministry. It is God's plan, purpose, and desire for you as individuals and as a church to be living in, and living out, this power placed upon your life daily. However, due to the issues within the church, this power was being greatly hindered, which is interesting, because as you read the letter to the Corinthians, the church really thought they were experiencing God's power to the fullest. As matter of fact, they even boasted to this end.

It would overwhelm us to discover the amount of men and women, and church congregations that believed they were living out and experiencing the power of God to the fullest. More amazing would be the amount of churches believed that their days of experiencing God's power to the fullest were behind them, though they might not openly admit it. In both circumstances, we see believers falling victim to the deceit of the enemy.

You can take these two points to the bank: 1) you have not, nor will you ever, experience the power of God to the fullest. He is omnipotent, which means there is no limit to His power. So just when you think you have seen Him do all that He can do, He does something more remarkable. Satan desires us to believe we are getting all of God because He understands just how much is there; and believe me, he is trembling! 2) God never changes. God does not begin something and not see it to completion. The thing that God began in you, or that God began in your church, will not be completed until the day of Christ's coming. The dry season you are experiencing may be because you are limiting God through your negative mindset, or you are limiting God through your lack of obedience.

Can you imagine how Paul's prayer must have stirred up the feelings of empowerment within these believers? The joy and peace they once knew, more than likely, began to fill their hearts and minds once again. They would have been reminded of their need to live holy, set apart lives for God. They would have realized that even though they were in the midst of sin, God could bring them out and God could still, and would still, use them. It must have stirred them to the place of repentance, to the place where they would become the people that God had called them to be from before the foundation of the world.

Can you imagine the impact your prayers, patterned the way Paul prayed, could have on your family? Friends? Co-workers? Church?

Are we honestly living out the calling that God has placed upon our lives? Are we, as individuals and churches, enjoying the peace and joy that flow from living out this call and knowing that we *are* called? Do you know anyone who has fallen away because of sin? Do you know anyone who is not experiencing the joy and peace? Maybe you have discovered that I am speaking directly to you, to your family, or to your church.

Let me encourage and affirm you today—God has called you, and God has a plan for your life. Come back home! You can begin by confessing and repenting of the sin that has hindered your walk with God. Then, pray that God will reconfirm within you His call for your life and that you will walk in the power of that calling. Pray like David, and ask God to restore unto you the joy of your salvation. Then, pray that God will lead you to someone else who has fallen away, and pray for them and encourage them, reaffirming the call that God has placed upon their life.

When you and I pray concerning the grace that others have received in Christ Jesus, we aid others in seeing the potential that God has placed upon their life. We help them remember that they have been called, that they have a purpose, and that they can, once again, experience the life that God intended for them from before the foundation of the world. Through this process, we recall what God has empowered us to do as well, and we will find our own lives remotivated to experience all that God has for us.

Chapter 5
Praying for Riches

I thank my God always concerning you for the grace of God which was given you in Christ Jesus, that in everything you were enriched in Him, in all speech and all knowledge.... (1 Cor. 1:5)

Through examining the prayer life of Paul, we are able to locate specific characteristics of prayer that can enable us to have more effective prayer lives. A more effective prayer life leads us to a place of discovering the power of God in and around us, yet, it also leads us to discovering the presence of God. A more effective prayer life will allow us to understand that God really is interested in what is happening in our lives. He is not only concerned about the crisis that we face; He is concerned about the mundane as well.

In thanking God for the believers, we have already seen the importance of thanking God for the work that others are doing for the sake of the Kingdom, and for the grace that the church received through Jesus Christ. When you and I become intentional in praying this way, we not only encourage others

34

in their walk with God, we recall what God has empowered us to do as well. This will lead to an overall transformation of the church to experience, again, all that God has for us.

From the previous chapter, we discussed that grace in the Bible can speak not only to the salvation received through Christ, but it can also speak to the empowerment or the equipment for ministry. In 1 Cor. 1:5, Paul thanks God for the grace that was given to the believers so they could do the ministry that they were empowered to do. Paul says that the believers at Corinth were enriched in Him (Jesus), in everything.

The term enriched literally means "to make rich." In some cases, this can denote material gain, but here it is used in the context of spiritual riches. If you are a believer, you are made rich through Christ! That is an exciting thought for me. I really like the way it sounds when I let it roll from my lips, "I am rich in everything through Christ!" Go ahead and try it for yourself. "I am rich in everything through Christ!" What does it mean to be rich in everything? I am glad you asked.

Let us consider the truth found in Col. 3:16, which states, "Let the word of Christ richly dwell in you, with all wisdom teaching and admonishing one another with Psalms and hymns and spiritual songs, singing with thankfulness in your hearts to God."

In the early church, the New Testament was not readily available. Actually, it probably would have been written on large scrolls of papyrus and, more than likely, chained to a lectern inside the synagogue. If the Word was going to be passed on to others, it needed to be memorized. Another interesting way the Word was passed on was through the singing of hymns. When Paul prayed that the word of Christ would richly dwell in this church, he was praying that they would memorize and pass on the very words of Jesus.

It was more than just memorizing the Word for knowledge however, Paul wanted the Word to richly dwell in these believers. What does it mean for that word to richly dwell in your life? What that means for you is that the hope that flows to you from the words of Christ would overflow within you, that the Word so fills you that it is literally busting at the seams to come out. You have tasted it, you are living it, you have been transformed by it, and you have to get it out to someone. I think we miss the power of God in our lives due to our lack of being saturated with the Word of God, and the willingness to share that Word with those we meet. Drink in the Word and then pour it out for others to hear.

An interesting scenario arises at this point. According to Col. 1:28, they were to be richly filled with the Word, and they were to take that Word to others so that every man who fell under the authority of the Word could be made perfect or would become mature in Christ. What I find interesting is that Paul encourages them to use Ps. and hymns to communicate God's truth. A psalm is simply Scripture that is set to music, preferably that of a stringed instrument. Here in the New Testament, we see Paul saying, take the Words of Christ, and add music to these words so that you may encourage those who need to hear.

Music has a tremendous role in our worship to God. In many cases, it sets the stage for the message that is about to come from the Word, and it allows the congregation to prepare their hearts to receive what God would have for them that day. It also communicates God's Scripture to our minds. I love to read the Psalms. and discover how many of our worship songs and praise chorus' find their roots in the Scripture. What a sad truth that many miss out on the role of music because they do not believe it has a place in the New Testament church. Friends, I see Paul in this verse telling us to use music to reach the world with the Words of Christ.

We are rich because the Words of Christ richly dwell in our lives! We must use that Word to minister to others!

The riches we find in Christ Jesus do not stop here. Paul shares a tremendously powerful truth for us in Rom. 2:4 when he states, "Or do you think lightly of the riches of His kindness and tolerance and patience, not knowing that the kindness of God leads to repentance?" (NASB)

We are rich! Part of this richness flows from the truth that, in His kindness, God holds back His judgment, giving people time to repent of their sins and return to Him. This is called grace! We do not deserve the extra time, yet God, in His kindness, tolerance, and patience, waits for us to come to Him. It is extremely difficult for us to expose our conduct to God and let Him tell us where we need to change. As believers, we must pray that God will point out *all* our sins, so that He can heal them. This is what David prayed in the Old Testament when he asked God to forgive him of all that he had done—those things that he knew about and those things that he had done without knowledge.

The riches that we have in Christ are divine attributes and are the gift of God to His people.

2 Cor. 8:9—Though Jesus was rich, He became poor, that we might become rich through Him.

Eph. 1:7—Redemption through His blood, and the forgiveness of sin according to His richness.

Eph. 3:4—We are rich in mercy and love wherewith He loved us.

Phil. 4:19—He shall supply every need according to His riches in glory in Christ Jesus.

Now, watch what happens to these verses when we consider what Paul says in Eph. 3:8, "Grace was given to me to preach the unreachable riches of Christ...."

This is amazing in context of what we are speaking to. The riches of Christ are unreachable. This means that they cannot be tracked out—they are unending. Therefore, when we say that we are rich through Christ, we have redemption and the forgiveness of sin according to His richness, we are rich in mercy and love, and He shall supply all our needs according to His riches; Paul is saying that there is absolutely no end to what Christ can do for us. Following this thought to completion, you have unending riches, redemption, forgiveness, mercy, love, and the ability to supply all your needs.

Not only is there no end to what Christ can do *for* you because of His riches, there is no end to what God can do *through* you either. This is the message Paul had for Corinth and the message He has for you and I! You have been called by the grace of God, and you have been made rich by the grace of God empowering you for the ministering of the Gospel. You may feel that your role is minor, and you may be right, but we forget the difference that God can make. I encourage you to draw on His richness, draw on His power, and fulfill the role that God has for you.

Paul continues this thought in 2 Cor. 9:11 when he says, "You will be enriched in everything for all liberality, which through us is producing thanksgiving to God."

You are rich! You are rich in liberality. You are rich in singleness or simplicity. God does not desire for your life to be complicated, and it is not His goal to make things more complicated for you. This is why Paul says you are rich in simplicity. Here it is, when you and I remain faithful to God and to the Words of Christ, which He has placed within us, He will direct our path and allow us to focus on what is important. If you are focused on what is important—God and His Kingdom, passing the Word on to others, and being equipped for ministry—your life will be full of thanksgiving.

In everything, the believers at the church in Corinth were enriched in Christ, in all speech (utterance) and all knowledge. In this prayer, Paul is thanking God for the power that was given to the church to speak out for God and to understand His truth.

If you trace through the Scripture you will find that the two words, speech and knowledge, are often linked together. When Paul is listing the gifts of the Spirit in 1 Cor. 12:8, he says that some receive words of wisdom, knowledge and healing are all given by the same Spirit. The purpose behind this can be seen through Eph. 4:12, "We are given these gifts for the perfecting of the saints and the building up of the body."

The speech that they were rich in was their means of testifying for Christ. They were using their words through

Scripture and singing Ps. and spiritual hymns. This church was verbally expressing their praise! I feel this is one area in which the church and believers struggle; as a result of our silence, we are lacking the power of God. He has given us the gift of words of wisdom for the building up of those around us, why do we then still refuse to lift up our voices?

One main reason I have found is many people feel as if they could not speak in front of people. They feel as if they may not have anything worthwhile to say. You are rich in speech. You are rich in praise! Therefore, stop worrying about the presentation and focus on the content, which is God and His unsearchable riches, and praise Him!

These believers were also rich in knowledge. Their knowledge was not found in books or held in degrees, the knowledge of these believers found God as its object. The things this church thought about revolved around God, and who He is. For this, they were rich. We need to follow this example. How easy it is to lose focus. How easy it is for us to allow our minds to be filled with things other than God. This is why the church is not busting forth at the seams with the Words of Christ. Most of the church is not interested in focusing on God. This is truly sad when you think that an unending supply is waiting for you, me, and our church, if we would just get our priorities where they should be. I am not sure how much clearer this truth could be than when Jesus says in Matt. 6:33, "Seek first the kingdom of God and His righteousness, and all these things will be added unto you." Think about God, let your mind revolve around God, and you will be rich!

Here, in a tightly wrapped package, is what Paul is communicating through this prayer of thanksgiving for the believers in Corinth. I know that you are struggling, and that there are problems beginning to rise within the church. Still, I am going to thank God for you. I am going to thank God, and hope you realize that you are spiritually rich. You are allowing the Words of Christ to be passed along to others through your testimony and witness. You are experiencing the patience of

God by receiving time to repent of your sin and time to know His grace and forgiveness. Although you have complicated things, God is trying to bring you back to the simple life in Christ.

Paul then continues by thanking God for the gift of speech and knowledge being given to this church. Have you ever wondered why Paul only mentions these two gifts? Simply put, these were the gifts that this church was to use specifically to build up, encouraging the body in the midst of what they were experiencing. They were to move on in love through giving of themselves even in the midst of their trials. This church was so focused on what was happening within the church, it would have been easy for them to lose sight of what was important. Yet they were being encouraged to allow God to be the center of their life.

Who do you know that is going through a hard time right now and could use a word of encouragement? Now, here is a hard question, are you allowing the Words of Christ to be passed along through you? Are you encouraging them through song or praise? I would hope that you would be found encouraging and building up those around you. If not, it is not too late to begin living out the gifts God has placed in your life.

Do you, or does someone you know, make the Christian life more difficult than God intended for it to be? If we are not careful, we can become very legalistic in our religion. We can place demands on others, and even demands upon ourselves, without even realizing it. The problem with these demands, which most of the time are not Biblical, is that we can never live up to them, so we always fall short. It is like people who come down on themselves for missing a Bible reading. They think that God does not feel the same about them due to missing this Bible reading. The truth is, our relationship with God is not based on what we do, it is based on placing our faith in Christ. That is it. Let us make an attempt to simplify our walk with God.

I would encourage you to take action and follow the example of the Apostle Paul if you want to receive more power in your life and see more power in your prayers. Begin praying, specifically, that God would lead you to someone this next week who needs to be encouraged in his or her own walk with Christ, and then encourage him or her. Pray that you stay focused on what is important, and when you feel your focus starting to drift, realign your priorities so you can experience His unending supply. Finally, pray that even if you are in the midst of a crisis that you will continue to practice the gift of giving, so that love will be manifest throughout your life and in the lives of others. You cannot underestimate the power of self-giving even when you feel as if there is nothing left to give. God's ability to use your life is unending.

Therefore, use your gift of speech and knowledge to encourage and build up those around you. Encourage those who are struggling to continue to see what is going on outside of their circle and make themselves available to help others. Allow God to be the center of your life. As a result, you will need to prepare yourself to experience a new level of power and a newfound reality of the presence of God.

Chapter 6
Praying for Confirmation

I thank my God always concerning you for the grace of God which was given you in Christ Jesus, that in everything you were enriched in Him, in all speech and all knowledge, even as the testimony concerning Christ was confirmed in you.... (1 Cor. 1:6) (NASB)

Throughout this study, we have been discussing ways that will enable us to have a more effective prayer life. An effective prayer life is essential in any believer who desires to experience God to the fullest during this life. A more effective prayer life leads to the ability to discover the power of God. After all, when we call upon God, we are asking Him to do something that we feel incapable of doing ourselves. We are calling upon Him and telling Him that we need Him to move, personally, in our lives—to change what needs to be changed, to intervene in the inevitable, and to make the crooked straight. Without an effective prayer life, the power of God will remain a complete mystery to us. With an effective prayer life, that same power, though we may not ever understand it completely, begins to take shape and drives us to want more of God.

An effective prayer life also leads to us discovering the presence of God in our lives. When we call out to God, we are asking Him to step into our situation, to walk alongside of us, and to comfort or to shelter us in His wing. Without a prayer life that is effective in reaching the heart of God, we will never know the joy, or the peace, or the contentment that comes from feeling the Savior pulling up beside us and saying, "Peace, be still." True, we will never know the full experience of being in the presence of God until that day when we see Him face-to-face. Through an effective prayer life, you will get a taste of what it is like to be with God, and this will drive you to want more of God.

Finally, a more effective prayer life leads us to discover that God really is interested in what is happening in our lives. You see, when you pray to the Creator of the universe, and He answers and changes your lot in life, you know He cares. An effective prayer life allows you to see God as more than just a judge sitting on His throne waiting to condemn you. An effective prayer life allows you to see God as He really is, a compassionate Father, a friend, a force that can make a real difference in your life. Without an effective prayer life, you will not have the joys of knowing that you are special to God. However, if you choose to pattern your prayers after those of the Apostle Paul, your prayer life will become more effective and you will see that you are important to God. With this knowledge released in your life there is nothing that you will not be able to do for God, because you will realize there is nothing God is not willing to do for you!

In three selected verses from 1 Cor. 1, Paul shares with us some tremendous lessons from his own heart and his own prayer life that led to effectiveness. It would do us well to recap, briefly, what we have learned so that we may be able to receive the full impact of the Scripture in the concluding verse.

In verse 4, Paul thanks God for the grace that the believers at Corinth had received. This prayer showed the believers at Corinth that they still belonged to God, and that God still had a purpose and a plan for their lives even though they may not be measuring up fully to the standards set before them. This leads us to consider whether or not we were living out the calling (plans and purposes) that God has placed on our lives. It furthermore leads us to realize the importance of helping others to see the grace of God that they have received, and to encourage them to live out the call God has placed on their life.

Following up in verse 5, Paul thanks God that even though these believers had fallen short, they were still called, and were even made rich in Jesus Christ. The richness that filled their lives found its roots in the words of Christ that dwelled within their hearts. They were also rich in God's kindness, tolerance, and patience. Finally, they were rich in the fact that they had made their faith simple. Paul goes on in this verse to thank God for the speech and the knowledge expressed by the church at Corinth. He encouraged them to use their gifts to help their brethren, to let them know that God had given them time to repent, and to call them back from the complicated system of religion to a fulfilling relationship in Christ.

We were able to find encouragement in this prayer to build up those around us, helping them to see their potential in Christ to encourage others as well. This reminds me of the advice that, as a pastor, I gave to a woman who came to visit me. Her husband had suffered a stroke, and for many years, she had given of herself to care of him and her children. She came to my office broken, not understanding why she had been chosen to experience this lot in life. I told her that God always allows us to experience things in this life to help others who are going through the same difficulties. It is amazing how God worked through this. A few days later, another woman who was going through the same thing visited me. Only she was ready to walk away. I was able to get these two women together and they shared their experiences with one another, drew strength from each other, and today both women are still living the lives that God has called them to with drive and purpose. We are called to build up those around us, and we are called to make God the center of our life.

Now, we come to verse 6, where Paul continues to offer up thanks for these believers. Here we see him thanking God for the testimony of Christ that was confirmed in their lives. The Apostle Paul wrote some strong words of correction to the Corinthian church, but in this one instance his words are strong, encouraging, and for a purpose. You see, it helps, when we are correcting others, to begin by affirming what God has already accomplished in them. For this church, it was the known reality of their spiritual gifts.

For Paul, the testimony of Christ was the witness of his preaching.

> For our gospel did not come to you in word only, but also in power and in the Holy Spirit and with full conviction; just as you know what kind of men we proved to be among you for your sake. (1 Thess. 1:5) (NASB)

Paul, Silas, and Timothy preached the gospel to the church at Thessalonica, and these believers were able to see that the message was true because they were living it out in the full power of the Holy Spirit. In other words, their testimony of Christ was confirmed among men, just as the church in Corinth.

When we tell others about Christ, we must depend on the Holy Spirit to open their eyes and convince them of their need. Without the working of the Spirit of God, our words and the things we do are meaningless. Our words and works are made manifest through the gifts and talents that the Holy Spirit gives to us. Paul, Silas, Timothy, and the church at Corinth were seeing tremendous results because they were putting into practice what the Holy Spirit had given them. Perhaps this is where we lack power in our prayer lives. We are praying that God will save people, we are praying that God will use us, and we are praying that God will do a mighty work. These are all good requests, however, if you are not using what God has given you to use, no wonder you are not seeing answers to your prayers and power in your life.

Paul tells the believers at Corinth that the testimony of Christ had been confirmed in them. The word confirmed means "to make a stand or to make stable." So, how was this word confirmed? By the gifts that this church had received. The very fact that the Holy Spirit had so lavishly imparted gifts and talents upon this church was confirmation that Christ dwelt in the hearts of the believers. Friends, the same is true for you and me. If you have received Christ as your Savior, you have been gifted by the Holy Spirit to do the work of Christ upon this earth. To each one is given the manifestation (American Standard Version) or gift of the Spirit. The Spirit distributes to each one individually as He wills. Each gift is given to build up or encourage the church, and to lead to the salvation of those without Christ.

To some He wills the gift of words of wisdom. Wisdom is intelligence with practical action. Here, specifically, it represents speech that is full of God's wisdom. Paul speaks to this in 1 Cor. 2 when he says, "But we speak God's wisdom in a mystery, the hidden wisdom which God predestined before the ages to our glory." To be full of words of wisdom means to communicate to others that God is offering His salvation to all people. Another gift that flows hand-in-hand with this is the words of knowledge. This is the gift of insight or illumination, or better, it is the ability to make all men see the light. Therefore, with the first gift you communicate that salvation is to all men, and with the second gift, you lead all men to see and accept the truth that Christ is for them.

To others the Holy Spirit imparts the gift of faith. Do not be confused by this, as every believer has faith, but not every person has the gift of faith, as this is a special gift. To have the gift of faith is to have an unusual measure of trust in the Holy Spirit's power. It is the ability to have faith and trust God when all others have given in or quit. It belongs to those who are visionaries, who can see and believe that with God, all things are possible. To put it simply, it is what you and I would call "wonder-working faith."

> If I have the gift of prophecy, and know all mysteries and all knowledge; and if I have all faith, so as to remove mountains, but do not have love, I am nothing. (1 Cor. 13:2)

> If you have faith the size of a mustard seed, you will say to this mountain, move from here to there, and it will move; and nothing will be impossible to you. (Matt. 17:20)

> If you have faith and do not doubt, you will not only do what was done to the fig tree, but even if you say to this mountain, be taken up and cast into the sea, it will happen. (Matt. 21:21)

The interesting thing about people who have been gifted with this Spiritual gift is that most other people avoid them; men and women who have the gift of faith are intimidating to many people. This type of faith makes those who are complacent in their walk with God uncomfortable. This faith, found in others, reveals our own level of faith and, for most, when we are found lacking, we remove ourselves under our own conviction. My suggestion to you is two-fold, 1) if you are the person who has been gifted with this particular gift, keep on dreaming, keep on believing, keep on praying, and keep on moving mountains. Do not allow the apathy of those around you to stop you from becoming all that God wants you to become. Do not stop believing in what God has placed within you, and 2) if you know someone who has been blessed with this gift, cling to them with all your might. Pray with them, visit with them, worship with them, and counsel with them. You will find that the more you saturate yourself with their company, the more the Spirit will pour off of them and onto you, and you may be surprised at how your opinion of what God can do in your life and through your life will change.

An active gift given by the Spirit of God is the gift of healing—put simply, it is the act of healing those who are sick or afflicted. I stated that this gift is active. The reason for this is many have lost the reality that God still heals! If our God is unchanging, and if His power is unchanging, then we have to believe that He still heals, and yes, He may use us as His agent of healing.

> While you extend your hand to heal and sign,
> and wonders take place through the name of
> Your Holy Servant Jesus. (Acts 4:30)

Healing through the laying on of hands was a consistent confirmation of the power of the Spirit being present. The healing did not come from Man, it came, and still comes, from God. The healing did not happen because of the faith of the sick, healing happened because of the faith of those doing the praying! Healing comes because there are people who still believe that God can do anything. Remember, if you believe, and ask, all things are possible. I was asked not long ago why some people or movements see God's healing power more than others? My answer to that is simple, "we have not because we ask not."

Along the same line as healing, some are given the gift of miracles. This is the working of powers to perform signs and wonders and special powers. These powers do not come from Man, they come from the Spirit of God which lives within (Gal. 3:5). When these miracles happen, they do not happen in order to elevate the man, they happen to testify of Christ and to confirm the presence of His Spirit. They do not happen because we want them to; they happen to fulfill God will on this earth.

> God also testifying with them, both by signs and
> wonders and by various miracles and by gifts of

the Holy Spirit according to His own will. (Heb. 2:4)

To others the gift is of prophecy. This is the ability to speak forth of things that one would not ordinarily know, and have them confirmed as truth. It speaks of preaching the Word of God with power, and giving God's message under the guidance of the Holy Spirit. How we need more with the gift of prophecy! When the Word of God is preached with power, we see results, and the results that we see are physical. My fear is that instead of preaching with power, we are simply delivering a motivational speech or a well-rehearsed lecture. Some have said that things are happening, but we just can't see what God is doing. Maybe so, but every time the Spirit of God fell through Holy Men of God in the New Testament, there was visible evidence and there was change! My prayer is that more would fall upon their knees and pray that God would give them the gift of prophecy, to be able to preach the Word under the power of the Holy Spirit and see God do things. What do we want God to do? Miracles, signs, wonders, and healing! We want to see God do things that will shake up our churches and our world, all for the glory and honor of God.

An important gift that is not always mentioned, is that of the distinguishing of spirits. This gift brings with it the ability to tell whether the gifts that people were exercising were really of the Holy Spirit and supernatural, or that devised in the heart of Man.

Beloved, do not believe every spirit, but test the spirits to see whether they are from God, because many false prophets have gone into the world. (1 John 4:1)

Unbelievably, there are some who will attempt to produce seemingly remarkable movements of the Spirit for their own gain or benefit. This may surprise you, but not everyone is interested in the welfare of others. There are many who have lied, and there will be others who lie, as long as our Lord tarries His return. We need men and women who have this gift to stand up, step forward, and expose false prophets. We need them to protect those who have been taken advantage of or those who are in danger of following a lie.

Probably the most debatable and controversial gift given by the Spirit is that of the gift of tongues. Let me say this from the outset, I do not have a problem with the gift of tongues, as long as it is done in a Biblical manner! This is where the controversy begins. Paul clearly teaches that when tongues are exercised it shall be done by two or, at the most, three people, and there should be someone present in the meeting who can interpret the tongue so that the whole church can receive edification from the words spoken (1 Cor. 14:27). If there is no one there to interpret, than the one speaking the tongue should remain silent. Again, I am aware that this stance is controversial in our day and time, however it is Biblical, and I believe that if we are going to experience all that God has for us, we must align our lives with the truth that is found in Scripture.

Clearly, there was a problem within the church at Corinth that resulted from the gifts that the Spirit had issued to all people. Paul tells us that everyone in the church was seeking the gift of tongues. The problem with this is that they were all members of one congregation, and we know that all the entities in the body cannot do the same thing if the body desires to function correctly. We also know that each person was given a specific function to carry out by the Holy Spirit for the good of the body. Paul addresses these misguided desires by listing the gifts in order of importance:

1) Apostles
2) Prophets
3) Teachers
4) Miracles
5) Healing

6) Helps (This would be the ministry or the office of the deacon, whose primary task it was to minister to the sick and needy of the church.)
7) Administration (This gift was typically found in the elders or bishops and in the outstanding leaders of the church.)
8) Tongues. (Notice that the gift everyone desired, Paul lists as last in order of importance.)

Paul concluded his teaching on spiritual gifts by saying we should earnestly desire the greater gifts, yet in the same breath he says that he will show them a supremely excellent way other than tongues or any of the other gifts mentioned. This way is the way of love (1 Cor. 13). The truth that Paul is conveying to this church, and to us as well, is simple, you desire to have these gifts and talents, and you are even envious of others gifts and talents. This desire comes from your need to be seen and accepted on a "spiritual" level. The problem is if you do not have love, and are not exercising your gift in the spirit of love, then you are just making a lot of noise and are not being effective for the Kingdom of God.

So in this particular portion of our study, Paul is thanking God for the spiritual gifts that had been given to the believers at the church in Corinth, and he is thanking God for their exhibition of these gift. The fact that they had received the gifts and were exercising them confirmed the fact that they indeed belonged to Christ. These gifts that had been received were given to help them and others to remain strong in faith.

What gifts has God given to you through His Holy Spirit? Just as important, are you using the gifts for your own edification or for the edification of the church? These are hard questions needing serious consideration, especially for leaders in the church. Are you doing what you do for the benefit of the Kingdom of God, or are you looking to see your career advanced or your status within the congregation solidified? An important concept that you should consider when answering these hard questions is that the effectiveness of your prayer life depends on you being honest with God. Perhaps the reason you are not experiencing more power in your prayers is because your petitions are being asked with selfish (whether realized or not) motives.

Here is something else for you to consider—do you know someone who God has obviously gifted? Is this individual using their gift, or do they need to be encouraged to exercise their gift for the glory of God? We see this all the time in churches across the country. Men and women are filing in the doors and filling the pews, and they are not utilizing the gifts that God has given to them. What they do not realize is that the church they worship in, and the church they love, will never be complete until they step up and fill their role in the body. It is your responsibility to encourage them to step up and put their gift into practice for the advancement of the Kingdom of God.

Let me share a testimony addressing this with you. There was a woman in a church where I pastored who was an exceptional flute player and obviously had the gift of making music. The unfortunate thing was that people in her family told her that her talent was not a gift and that God could not use her talent in the church. The interesting thing about this is that our church had a small ensemble that played music each week to accompany our choir. This woman stopped me as I was entering the sanctuary one Sunday morning and asked what I thought about her dilemma. She really wanted to play but was being discouraged by those close to her. My words were brief and to the point, I told her that her talent *was* a gift and that she should not allow anyone to stand in the way of her using that gift for the advancement of the Gospel message. She told me she was glad that I felt the way she did, and she pulled out her flute, sat down to play, and she continues to play her heart out for the Lord each and every week.

At this point, I encourage you to set this book down and do some serious reflection. Ask God to make it clear to you what your gifts and callings are in this life for His Kingdom. Then pray that God will give you the opportunity to use your gift and calling. In essence, ask God to guard your heart and your motives for using your gifts, and that it will not be for attention or selfish gain, but it will be for the advancement of His Kingdom. Finally, pray that God will lead you to someone that you can encourage in exercising their gifts and talents as well.

Chapter 7
Praying for Love

For this reason I too, having heard of the faith in the Lord Jesus which exists among you and your love for all the saints, do not cease giving thanks for you, while making mention of you in my prayers. (Eph. 1:15–16) (NASB)

As we continue to study the prayers of the Apostle Paul, we find him offering up thanks for the believers at the church in Ephesus. He says that he has heard of their faith in the Lord Jesus, and he has heard of their love for all the saints. He mentions that he does not cease to give thanks for them during his time before the Lord.

When Paul wrote the letter to the Ephesians, he wrote to give them an in-depth teaching on how to nurture and to maintain unity within the church. How we need this lesson in our churches today! Without love, it is impossible for a church to stay unified. Let me go further and say that without love it is impossible for any relationship to function properly. The interesting thing about Paul's address to this church is that he does not say he is writing to the believers "in Ephesus." What is so special about this, you may be wondering? It is believed that this letter first circulated to the church at Ephesus and then, because of the nature and importance of the words penned by Paul, its message continued on to the other churches impacted by the ministry of Paul. In short, this is not a centralized message sent to address a problem in one specific congregation. It was a message sent to address a problem that all the churches were experiencing, and continue to experience—unity.

We can learn a great deal from the history of the church at Ephesus, and, by understanding this history, we can better understand the message. Ephesus was one of the five major cities in the Roman Empire. Paul visited the city while traveling on his second missionary journey (Acts 18:19–21). The city itself was a commercial, political, and religious center for all of Asia Minor. The city was also the home of the temple dedicated to the Roman goddess Artemis (Greek: Diana), which is one of the Seven Wonders of the Ancient Wonders. I have visited the replica of this temple in Nashville, Tennessee, and it is an amazing and intimidating display as you look up to the eleven-story-tall statue of the goddess. The temple, being in the Ephesus, proved to be troublesome for Paul's ministry as a major industry in the city was the manufacturing of images of Artemis (Acts 19:21–41). While Paul ministered in this city, he warned the Eph. against false teachers who would come in and try to draw the people away from their faith. Both Paul and John testify that the believers here were able to resist these teachers.

To have a clearer understanding of the character found in the lives of the believers within this church, the character that Paul thanked God for being found in their lives, we need to examine the passage found in Rev. 2:1–7. John gives us a great deal of insight into this church. Verse 1 teaches us that Ephesus had become a large and powerful church, and the message that Jesus had for them would be an attempt to remind them that, in the midst of their growth, Jesus alone is the head of the church. Following, in verse 2, we see Jesus himself commending them for working hard, persevering in the midst of both temptation and persecution, and resisting sin. The church at Ephesus also critically examined the claims expressed by the false apostles and endured hardships without becoming weary.

The interesting thing about this church is not only did they resist sin, but they did not tolerate sin in the lives of its members. How we need to follow their example, especially on this issue! When church members tolerate sin in the church, they are lowering their standards, and compromising their witness in the community and in the world. We have to come to a place where we do all we can to not offend. The truth is that when we know that a brother or sister is living in sin, we are told to go to them and to encourage them to repent of that sin and turn back to Christ. When we worry about tenure in the church, or tithes paid to the church, more than the call to holiness, we are worried about the wrong things and we are sure to hinder God's work in our churches. Perhaps this is what has led to the dying off of many denominational churches. Instead of addressing or taking care of the sin that is in our camp, we have allowed it to survive, in the name of tenure or tithes, and we are being eaten away from the inside out. Praise God for a church that holds itself and its members accountable for the lives that live in Christ Jesus.

What a wonderful time we would have in the house of God each week if every church had the same qualities that were found in the church at Ephesus. How blessed we would be if our efforts to live and serve rightly were rooted in love, as was this church. This is precisely what Paul is thanking God for in verses 15 and 16, and this is what Jesus was confirming in Rev. 2:4, even though by this time the church had stopped loving.

Both Jesus and John stressed that having love for one another was authentic proof that the Gospel of Christ had transformed your life.

John 13:34–35 — A new commandment I give to you, that you love one another, even as I have loved you, that you also love one another. By this all men will know that you are My disciples, if you have love for one another.

The new commandment comes from the radical way Jesus was commanding them to love one another. Friends, love will bring even unbelievers to Christ. Millions of people are waiting to experience genuine love. Not love because of what they have to offer, or because they look just like us, but love and acceptance just as they are, where they are. They are waiting to be loved by people like you! When you choose to open your heart and love them with the same love that was expressed to you from Christ, you are also opening up the door for them to accept Christ's love as well. I believe one reason more people are not coming into the church or into the family of Christ is that they have been made to feel as if Christ would not love them. Can you guess where they got the idea? From the very men and women Christ left upon this earth to be his hands and feet. If they do not feel love and acceptance from you, they will not seek it from Christ. The church at Ephesus was commended for their love, and guess what, the church at Ephesus grew.

Love also keeps believers strong and united in a world that is hostile to God. As believers, we have enough enemies and naysayers. We have enough battles to face on a daily basis, so getting along with one another should not be an issue. If we find that we have different ideas or differences of opinion, that is good and to be expected. However, our position in Christ should keep us unified and heading in the right direction. Nothing today stifles the work of God quicker than believers who cannot coexist with one another. Most times what happens is that one party will leave the church with issues unresolved, carry their burden to another church, and then disrupt the harmony there. Meanwhile, the person left behind is never truly happy. Sure, their problem is gone, but they never have closure, and therefore their level of acceptance and love is not what it should be. If we are ever going to follow the pattern of

Paul, we must learn from this church in Ephesus, and we must apply the teaching of Jesus, John, and Paul. We have to learn to love one another so that as a body, we can be unified, and as a body, we can be strong.

Something amazing happens when we learn to love like Christ. Immediately, we are cast before the eyes of the world as living examples of His love. People are drawn to others who they see do not have a problem with loving others. If they constantly hear you complaining, murmuring, or nagging, they will not share with you. As a result, they will not see Christ in you, which will cause them to shy away. Yet, if they observe your actions and if your words are appropriate, they are pulled in by the difference they see in you. They will know that you are special and that you belong to Christ, and the tremendous thing about this is they will want what you have! I am thoroughly convinced that the church at Ephesus grew because they knew how to love and were not divided over petty issues that were not important.

We must pause to insure that all who are reading this book will understand a very real truth about the kind of love of which I speak. In context of our teaching, the love that I am speaking of is more than just a word spoken between two people. The love that I, and the authors of Scripture, am speaking of, results in action. It is helping when it is not convenient for you. It involves the concept of giving even while you are hurting. It is energy that is devoted to the welfare of others. It is absorbing hurts from others without complaining or fighting back. I once heard someone say that, "true love is doing what is best for the other person, regardless of what it costs you." This is the way Jesus loved, and this is the same love that He calls us to live out as we follow Him.

Honestly, it is not an easy task to love this way; it is hard, and it will cost you something. However, nothing worthwhile is ever cheap or easy. The effort you put into loving others is the reason why people notice when you do it. Loving God and loving others is the most important thing that the Christ follower can do. It is more important than all the spiritual gifts exercised within the church today. It is love that makes our actions and gifts useful, and this same love that is available to everyone; our gifts are not.

Consider the words of the Apostle Paul as he describes what love is in 1 Cor. 13:1–8.

> If I speak the language of men and of angels, but do not have love, I am a sounding gong or a clanging cymbal. If I have the gift of prophecy, and understand all mysteries and all knowledge, and if I have all faith, so that I can move mountains, but do not have love, I am nothing. And if I donate all my goods to feed the poor, and if I give my body to be burned, but do not have love, I gain nothing. Love is patient; love is kind. Love does not envy; is not boastful; is not conceited; does not act improperly; is not selfish; is not provoked; does not keep a record of wrongs; finds no joy in unrighteousness, but rejoices in the truth; bears all things, believes all things, hopes all things, endures all things. (Holman Christian Standard Bible)

Let's also take a quick look together at what John has to say about love in 1 John 3:18–19.

> Little children, let us not love with word or with tongue, but in deed and truth. We will know by this that we are of the truth, and will assure our heart before Him. (NASB)

This is the very reason that we find Paul thanking God for this church. The believers in Ephesus were demonstrating this type of love. I would venture to say this church was unified, and I would also venture to say they were having an impact in their community. The sad side of this story is realized in Rev. 2:4.

But I have this against you: you have abandoned
the love you had at first.

At one moment, Paul is thanking God for them, and
then we see Jesus' message to John about this church. What
happened? How did they go from being a loving congregation
to a congregation who left their first love? Follow the transition
and take note, as we see this happening in churches all around
our country. The church at Ephesus suffered because many of
the church founders had died, and the second generation of believers lost their zeal and enthusiasm for God and the things of
God. Although these Christians were still abounding in the
work of the Lord, they were doing the work with the wrong
motives. Take note; work done for God must be motivated out
of love for God and others or it will not last!

I would also like to comment on the spiritual shift of
the second generation of believers because, if we are not careful, this shift can happen in our lives as well. Have you noticed
that when a person first makes the decision to become a Christian they are filled with enthusiasm? They do not have a lot of
knowledge about the Bible or doctrines or theology, but they
have Jesus, and for them, that is enough. Their love for Jesus
propels them to love others and to do the work of God so that
they can see the Kingdom of God grow.

As time goes on, these same enthusiastic Christians begin to attain more knowledge about the Bible—they begin to
understand more about doctrine and theology. Before long, the
enthusiasm that once drove them is replaced by knowledge.
Now, they want sermons that better clarify the Word of God,
they the Word expounded to them so they will be intellectually
stimulated. Church services become about what they like and
what will fulfill their desires. The sad thing is that seeing the
Kingdom grow, although it is theologically and doctrinally cor-
rect, is not the main agenda.

Friends, if you are going to thrive for the Kingdom of
God, if you are going to be a God-chaser or Christ-follower,

may I say that you need a healthy dose of both enthusiasm and knowledge! Enthusiasm and knowledge combined will lead the Christian to both understand their purpose here on earth, and be excited and challenged to fulfill that purpose. If we are not careful to maintain a healthy balance of both, it is possible that we will find ourselves in the same position as the church at Ephesus. Having left our first love, instead of being commended by Christ, we just may be condemned!

Consider taking the time right now to ask yourself some very important questions. Remember to be completely honest with yourself while answering, as this will be the only way you can move back in line with what God wants for your life. Are you motivated by love in the things that you do for God, or does your motivation stem from what you have to gain or because there is no one else to do it? Is your church motivated by love? Is your church unified? Remember, unity does not always mean an absent of conflict. It carries with it the idea that you are going forward together in the same direction for the glory of God. Do you have a healthy balance between your level of enthusiasm and knowledge? Have you lost your zeal?

I encourage you to take the time to cover these questions and pray upon the basis of your answers. I ask you to pray that you, personally, will begin to love others the way Christ loved you. How did He love you? He did what was best for you, regardless of what it cost Him. He gave His live so that you could find yours. I ask you to pray that your church, and churches across our area, will love each other. Finally, I ask that you pray to become more passionate about Christ, more passionate about the things of Christ, and more passionate about the work of Christ.

It is amazing, all that we can take and learn from a simple prayer of thanksgiving offered by the Apostle Paul on behalf of the church at Ephesus. My hope and prayer for you is that you will take what we have learned throughout this chapter and turn it from mere head-knowledge to an active part of your everyday life.

Chapter 8
Praying for Hope

We give thanks to God, the Father of our Lord Jesus Christ, praying always for you, since we heard of your faith in Christ Jesus and the love which you have for all the saints; because of the hope laid up for you in heaven, of which you previously heard in the word of truth, the gospel which has come to you, just as in all the world also it is constantly bearing fruit and increasing, even as it has been doing in you also since the day you heard of it and understood the grace of God in truth.... (Col. 1:;3-6) (NASB)

The book of Colossians is grouped together with three other books in the New Testament labeled The Prison Epistles. They are labeled as such because, when Paul penned them, he was being held in prison at Rome. The actual prison was a house where Paul was kept under close guard. He, most likely, would have been chained to a Roman soldier twenty-four hours a day. Paul was treated differently than most prisoners at this time in that he was afforded the luxury of seeing any visitors that he wanted to see, and he was allowed to write letters to people and to churches throughout the known world. Thus, we have our text.

The city of Colossae was located one-hundred miles east of the city of Ephesus. Colossae was an ancient city that found itself declining commercially. It was considered a city of crossroads for ideas and religions. There was also a very large Jewish population in the city. Many of these Jews fled from Jerusalem almost two-hundred years before Christ came to the earth under the persecution of Antiochus III & IV.

The church at Colossae was founded by Epaphras (Act 19:10), who was a hero to this church, and he is the one responsible for holding things together in spite of the growing persecution and struggle with false doctrines. His prayers show us the deep love he had for these people:

> Epaphras, who is one of your number, a bond slave of Jesus Christ, sends you his greetings, always laboring earnestly for you in his prayers, that you may stand perfect and fully assured in all the will of God. For I testify for him that he has a deep concern for you and for those who are in Laodicea and Hierapolis. (Col. 4:12-13) (NASB)

Church historians believed that Epaphras came to know Christ while he was in Ephesus. For reasons unknown to us, he visited Paul while he was imprisoned for the first time in Rome. It is also possible that Epaphras was in jail with Paul for preaching the Gospel. It would have been during one of these encounters that Epaphras shared with Paul the heresy that was found in the church, and Paul would have written his letter. As far as we know, the church itself met in the house of Philemon (Philem. 23).

Before we go any further in our search for power through prayer, it is important to quickly pass over some of the heresies this church was facing. Paul's praise of this church will have more meaning when we understand what they were going through. It is important for us to consider these things because they are some of the very heresies the church faces today. Although churches may have different names, the teachings and dangers are the same.

Heresy #1
The Spirit is good and matter is evil.

We need to understand that God is the creator of all things. When he created the heavens and the earth, He looked at them and said that it was good. All things were created for the glory of God. Matter only becomes evil as man, due to his sinful nature, takes what God has made, and twists it to fulfill his own lustful desires.

Heresy #2
One must follow ceremonies, rituals, and restrictions in order to be saved or perfected.

Let me be perfectly clear on this point: Christ is all one needs to attain salvation. There is nothing man can do to take away from, or add to, the sufficient offering that Christ made upon the cross of Calvary. Baptism, the Lord's Supper, church attendance and service, and money given do not ensure salvation. It is by grace through faith that we are saved, not of works lest any man should boast, it is a gift of God…. (Eph. 2:8–9)

Heresy #3
One must deny the body and live in strict asceticism.

Asceticism is the act of rejecting bodily pleasure through self-denial and self-mortification. The object was to strengthen oneself spiritually and was often practiced by priests and monks. It is practiced today as religious groups abstain from certain things in order to become more spiritual, for example, movies, dress, hair, and make-up. Asceticism offers no help in conquering evil thoughts and desires. Remember that Jesus taught us that sin begins in the heart! If we are to live for God, than we

64

must take care of the condition of our heart so our words and actions will align with Christ's plan for our life. Asceticism, more often than not, led to, and continues to lead to, a life of pride.

Heresy #4
Angels must be worshipped.

What I see in the church today is a total misunderstanding of angels. An entire chapter could be written on this, so to make it concise let me say this—people who die do not become angels, angels are created beings, and no angel was ever meant to be worshiped. The Bible is clear that the Holy Trinity, consisting of God the Father, God the Son, and God the Holy Spirit, alone are worthy of our worship.

Heresy #5
Christ could not be both human and divine
at the same time.

Christ is God as the flesh, He is the eternal One, He is the head of the body, the First in everything. Although it is hard for us to comprehend the aspect of Him being human as well as divine, we must realize that, in Him, was all the fullness of the Godhead in bodily form, while at the same time, He was completely human to be able to sympathize with the pain and trials we experience during this life.

Heresy #6
One must obtain "secret knowledge" in order to be saved
or perfected, and this knowledge is not available to
everyone.

Here is the mystery: Christ came to earth to die for all men! He is not willing to let even one person perish, and it is His desire for all to come to repentance. We make the decision not to come to Christ. Since we do not know who will and who will not make that decision, it is the responsibility of the church to share the Gospel of Christ with everyone.

Heresy #7
One must adhere to human wisdom, tradition, and philosophies.

As a Christian, we should live by what Christ taught in his Word as our ultimate authority. Sadly, if you are trusting in what Man teaches from his own philosophy or wisdom, you are going to be greatly disappointed in this life and in the life to come.

Heresy #8
It is better to combine aspects from several religions.

This is so relevant to the day and time we are living in. Forget chapters, I could write a whole book on religious pluralism and the idea that it doesn't matter how you get there as long as you get there.

Unfortunately for those who adhere to this type of thinking, they miss the truth that all they need, and all they want, can be fulfilled in Christ! He is all sufficient! Friends, that is why Christ came and died upon the cross, it was so we would no longer have to seek out different ways to get to God. We have one way, one truth, which leads to one life (John 14:6), and that it Christ!

Heresy #9
There is nothing wrong with immorality.

There *is* something wrong with immoral living as it leads you in the opposite direction of where God wants to take you. It destroys both your life and the lives of those you associate with, and no good can come from it.

The Bible encourages us to get rid of the sin and evil that we have in our hearts and in our lives because we have been chosen by God to live a new life as a representative of the Lord Jesus. This new life that we have been called to live involves making the right decisions based upon God's Word and living a holy, set-apart life.

In the midst of everything, this church is battling in their quest to advance the kingdom, and Paul wants them to know that he is praying for them. In Colossians 1:3, Paul lets the believers know that he is also thanking God for them. Following, verse 4 and 5 share with us what Paul is thanking God for.

> Col. 1:4–5, Since we heard of your faith in Christ Jesus and the love which you have for all the saints; because of the hope laid up for you in heaven, of which you previously heard in the word of truth, the gospel. (NASB)

Paul begins his praise of this church by thanking God for the faith that they have in Jesus Christ. This is a tremendous statement when you consider all the heresies this church was battling. Even those who were Christians were struggling with the idea that Christ alone was not the way of salvation, and many were searching for the special knowledge that led to eternal life. In the midst of this, Paul says, "thank you God for those who are being true to their faith in Jesus!"

I think you will find that the next two things Paul thanks God for go hand-in-hand. He wants to thank God that they have love for all the saints, and this love is motivated by the next thing Paul thanks God for, and that is the hope which they had laid up in heaven. This church had heard those wonderful words of life. They not only heard, but they believed and accepted them as well. What are the wonderful words of life? The Gospel of Jesus Christ!

Perhaps this is a good place for us to make sure everyone reading this book has heard and understands the Gospel of Christ. Because each person who is born into this world has the nature of sin, there is not one person who is able to do what is right and attain the favor of God (Rom. 3:10). This is the reason why, apart from Jesus, it is impossible for us to make it to heaven when we leave this earth (Rom. 3:23). So, because God understands our dilemma, He sent His only Son, Jesus, down to this earth to die on our behalf so that we could receive the forgiveness of sin that we needed in order to attain the favor of God and life eternal (Rom. 5:8). We cannot do anything on our own to inherit eternal life and, as a matter of fact, all the things that we do in our own strength merit death. God's gift of eternal life is free, and it comes by accepting Jesus Christ as our Savior and Lord (Rom. 6:23).

How does a person accept Christ as Savior and Lord? If you confess with your mouth that you have sinned, if you believe in your heart that Jesus is God's Son who came to this earth to die for your sins and that God raised him from the dead on the third day, then you will have eternal life (Rom. 10:9).

You may be thinking, "That is too easy, there has to be something else I need to do," or perhaps, "What about all the things I have done wrong in the past," or, "I do not know enough to have eternal life." Let me answer these thoughts for you, it was never meant to be hard! Eternal life is God's gift to you, and there is nothing more you need to do than to believe and trust in Jesus. Anyone, and that means you, who calls on the Lord will be saved (Rom. 10:13). All God asks you to know is that you need Jesus, that He is God's Son, and that He died for your sins.

How about it? Would you like to know that your sins have been forgiven and that you have an eternal home reserved for you in heaven? Why not pray to ask Christ to come into your heart right now. You can do it wherever you are reading this book. You can do it by praying a simple prayer such as the following:

> *Dear Jesus, I believe that you are God's Son and that you came to this earth to die upon the cross for my sins. Jesus, I am asking you right now to forgive me of all my past, present, and future sins. I am asking you to come into my heart and give to me the gift of eternal life in heaven. Amen.*

Friends, *that* is the Gospel message! If you prayed to receive Christ as your Savior, welcome to the family of God! Let me encourage you to find a good Bible-believing church and tell the minister at that church the decision you just made so that he can rejoice with you and help you grow in your new-found faith. Praise God!

This is what the believers at Colossae believed and hoped in, and the freedom that they received through Jesus Christ is what enabled them to love all the saints. When we learn and accept that our future is secure as a believer in Jesus Christ, then we become free to live for Christ and free to love others.

> 1 Pet. 1:3–4, Blessed by the God and Father of our Lord Jesus Christ, who according to His great mercy has caused us to be born again to a living hope through the resurrection of Jesus Christ from the dead, to obtain an inheritance which is imperishable and undefiled and will not fade away, reserved in heaven for you....(NASB)

I believe the point highlighted in verse 6 of Paul's prayer speaks volumes to us today. The Word that the believers had received in their own heart was the same word that was spoken to others throughout the world. Everywhere that the Word was spoken and received, fruit was produced. The impact of the receiving of the Word did not stop there, the fruit that was produced did not just remain, it increased and spread constantly.

When men and women come to Christ, a transition should take place in their life. There should be a change. As we enter into this new relationship with God, we receive a new purpose, a new direction, a new attitude, and a new form of behavior. The "new" that we put on after receiving Christ should result in the believer no longer living their life for themselves, but living their life so they bear fruit for the kingdom of God.

Let me pause at this point and speak to you from my heart. I have a hard time accepting a person as a true child of God when they refuse to, or do not, see any growth in their spiritual life. I believe the Word has clearly spoken on this issue. If you hear the Word and accept the Word, spiritual fruit will be produced. This fruit will lead to a greater desire to be like Christ, and to seek the things of Christ. What is it that Christ wants to see happen on this earth? The spreading of the Gospel message so men and women will be saved.

This leads to the second difficulty that I have. I cannot understand how a church, a body of believers, can ever be satisfied to remain the size that they are. I believe it should be the goal and purpose of every church to grow. I know the old adage that some people would rather attend a smaller church, but this is contrary to Scripture. Saying, I want to attend a small church, is the same as saying, I am not concerned with seeing men and women come to Christ. When you are living out the Gospel fully in your life, you will bear fruit. The result of that fruit will be for others to come to Christ, which naturally results in your church growing.

The church at Colossae, according to the way Paul prayed, obviously understood this point, because as believers, they were producing fruit, and as a congregation, they were spreading the Gospel all over, and for this Paul was offering up thanksgiving to God. How we can learn from their example? How we, as a body of believers, need to seek the things of Christ. How we need to come back to the place where it is our desire to see men and women saved. Your time in worship is not about what you like or desire, it should be about what will draw unchurched men and women into the house of God to hear the Word of God, and result in them entering into a personal relationship with God.

There is a final, interesting note that we discover in Colossians 1:3–5. We see the triad of Christian graces in the lives of these believers. In verse 4, Paul speaks of their faith and love, and in verse 5 he calls out their hope. We learn from the Apostle in 1 Cor. 13, that faith is the foundation and content of God's message, hope is the attitude and focus that the believer should possess, and love is putting our faith and hope into action. Friends, when your faith and hope are in line, you are able to love completely because you are interested in sharing God's love.

I believe, more than anything, that this is what led to the spiritual success of these believers. They had the faith and the hope, and lived them out in love. As a result, the Word was bearing fruit and spreading among them. Until the church is able to get these three graces in line, we will be barren and will not receive the growth, spiritually and numerically, that God has for us. When we are in line, the Spirit is free to move in us and among us, leading to you and me to experience great and mighty things in our personal lives and in the life of our individual congregations, and as the Kingdom whole.

Ask yourself some very important questions concerning the prayer Paul prayed for the believers at Colossae. Are you basing your hope in heaven on the Word of God or on the teachings and philosophies of man? Is your faith in Christ motivated by the hope that you have in heaven, which leads to you being more loving? Is the Word producing fruit in your life? Is that fruit leading you to spread the Gospel?

These are very personal and important questions to ask. Once you have made peace with your answer, begin to pray. If you have not yet asked Christ to come into your heart, pray to enter into a personal relationship with him. Pray that your hope in heaven will lead you to love others. Pray that you will begin to either grow, or continue to grow, in your Christian life. Pray that God will give you a burden for the unchurched in your life, and seek to see the church and the Kingdom of God grow.

If we apply the things Paul prayed in this prayer to our life and our walk with God, we will discover the power of God in our life. It will amaze you when you see what God wants to do in you and through you as His child.

Chapter 9
Praying for Fruit

1 Thess. 1:2–7

*We give thanks to God always for all of
you, making mention of you in our prayers; constantly bearing in mind your work of faith and
labor of love and steadfastness of hope in our
Lord Jesus Christ in the presence of our God
and Father, knowing, brethren beloved by God,
His choice of you; for our gospel did not come
to you in word only, but also in power and in
the Holy Spirit and with full conviction; just as
you know what kind of men we proved to be
among you for your sake. You also become imitators of us and of the Lord, having received the
word in much tribulation with the joy of the
Holy Spirit, so that you became an example to
all the believers in Macedonia and in Achaia.*
(NASB)

When you and I choose to follow the example of the
Apostle Paul's prayer life, it provides us with a pattern in

which we can pray for others. It allows us to see the importance of offering praise unto God for what God is doing, not only in our life, but also in the lives of those we minister with and to. Praying like Paul also provides us with insight into living a life for God that will make an impact in the world in which we live.

In this particular prayer, Paul is writing to the believers who were assembled in the church at Thessalonica. Thessalonica was the largest city and the capital of Macedonia, which boasted a population of near two-hundred thousand people. It was the home to the most important Roman highway, the Egnatian Way. This highway stretched from Rome all the way to the Orient. Thessalonica was also one of the wealthiest and most flourishing trade centers in the Roman Empire. An important note for us to remember is that Thessalonica was a free city, and this meant that they were allowed self-rule, and were exempt from most restrictions placed on other cities by the Rom.. It was also home to many pagan religions, which challenged the faith of the young Christians who were living there.

The church at Thessalonica was planted by Paul around AD 50. He did not spend much time here because his life was being threatened (Acts 17:1–10). When he arrived in Corinth after departing, he sent Timothy back to see how the young Christians were doing. Timothy returned to Paul with good news. He reported that they were remaining firm in their faith despite impending persecution, and that they were united as a body of believers. They did, however, have some questions; it was in response to these questions that Paul penned this Epistle.

As is custom with the writings of Paul, he begins with a greeting and turns right to giving thanks on behalf of this church to God by saying, "We give thanks to God always for you all making mention of you in our prayer." His message for you and me today begins in verses 3 and 4 when he states, "...constantly bearing in mind you work of faith and labor of love and steadfastness of hope in our Lord Jesus Christ in the presence of our God and Father, knowing, brethren beloved by God, *His* choice of you."

What an awesome testimony this young church produced. Paul was commending them for standing firm even when they were being persecuted. As believers we need to do more research and gain a better understanding of how believers are standing for Christ throughout the world despite persecution. Believers meet in secret with the threat of jail, and in some cases death, yet they do not hold back their praise. They are faithful to God despite what their faith in God may cost them. In America, we know very little about persecution or the threat of persecution, prison, or death for our faith. Perhaps this is why we are so apathetic in our worship, we feel as if we have nothing to lose or gain by our faithfulness and the zeal expressed to our heavenly Father. I know that was a bold statement to make. However, believers in Thessalonica and throughout the world, were, and are, making a difference worthy of praising God for, even in the midst of persecution. While here in America, the church is dying without the threat of persecution.

Paul also thanks God and commends the believers at Thessalonica for their work produced by faith, their labor prompted by love, and their endurance inspired by hope. Here is the triad of Christian Graces again. Let take a closer look at the following Scripture, which addresses each of these graces.

Their work produced by faith

> John 6:29, Jesus answered and said unto them, "This is the work of God, that you believe in Him whom He has sent." (NASB)

This particular Scripture answers the question, "What does God want me to do?" Friend, God wants us to believe of Jesus, whom God sent. We can do a lot in the name of God or in the name of religion, even a particular denomination or church, however, pleasing God does not come from the work we do, it comes from whom we believe in. Therefore, if you desire to please God with your life, the first step is to accept that Jesus is who he claims to be—the Christ, the Anointed One, the Messiah, and the Son of the Living God (Matt.16:16).

> Gal. 5:6, For in Christ Jesus neither circumcision nor uncircumcision means anything, but faith working though love.

Religious practices and traditions will not lead us to receiving the forgiveness of sin or inheriting a home in heaven. We are saved by grace through faith. Love for God and a love for others is the response of those who God has forgiven. Listen to the words of Jesus when he said, "Those who are forgiven must love much" (Lk 7:47). There is not a whole lot of wiggle room, is there?

> 1 Thess. 3:6, But now that Timothy has come to us from you, and has brought us good news of your faith and love, and that you always think kindly of us, longing to see us just as we also long to see you.

Another result of the faith that we have in Christ is our desire to be with our brethren. We will desire the companionship and fellowship of those who are like-minded with us. Our thoughts will also be different. Instead of thinking the way we did before we knew Christ, our faith will give us the ability to see people as they really are, and it will afford us the ability to cut them some slack when they do not live up to our expectation of them.

> 2 Thess. 1:3,"We ought always to give thanks to God for you, brethren, as is only fitting, because your faith is greatly enlarged, and the love of each on of you toward one another grows even greater.

This result rides piggyback with the one listed above. As children of God walking in faith, our desire to love each other grows continually. This love will find its root in the amount of love that was expressed towards us on the cross of Calvary. This love will overlook all the imperfections in the life of those we worship with, as well as our own. This love will lead to unity of mind and purpose within the body of Christ.

> 2 Thess. 1:11, To this end we pray for you always, that our God will count you worthy of your calling, and fulfill every desire for goodness and the work of faith with power.

Our faith in God will lead us to see the desires in our heart for ministry to become a reality. It may not come overnight, but if you are diligent in your efforts, God's hand of blessing will come upon your life, until one day you open your eyes and you realize that you are on your way. I cannot explain to you the release that comes when you know that you are walking God's perfect path for your life.

> James 2:17, Even so faith, if it has not works, is dead, being by itself.

Let me state this again, works do not result in your salvation. Your salvation is by grace through faith; however, your faith would, and should, be accompanied by works if it is real faith. When you and I live out our faith through deeds of loving service, we verify to a world that is always watching that our faith in Christ is real.

Their labor prompted by love

> Rom. 16:6, ...greet Mary who has worked hard for you....

Heb. 6:10, For God is not unjust so as to forget your work and the love which you have shown toward His name, in having ministered and in still ministering to the saints.

When doing the work of God, it is very easy for us to get discouraged—for us to think that no one is noticing the effort that we are putting into teaching or cleaning or serving. Paul reminded the saints to thank those people who continuously serve. Unfortunately, we do not always remember to heed this advice, and feelings get hurt and neglected. If you have found yourself in this position, do not lose heart! God sees everything that you are doing and the sacrifices that you are making and He will reward you. Sometimes that reward may come while you are here on this earth, but rest assured the reward *will* come when you stand before Him in heaven. God never overlooks what one of His children does for Him.

Their endurance inspired by hope

The believers of this church were eagerly anticipating the return of Christ. They believed in the promise of heaven, and they believed in the promise of eternal rest. This hope of experiencing a better day led them to be faithful through the midst of all they were enduring in this life. Church should be our encouragement today as well. In the midst of divorce rates climbing, the economy failing, liberal agendas spreading and apathy running wild, it would be easy for us to get discouraged and simply quit trying. Let me say this, keep on serving, keep on loving, and keep on keeping on for God! This world is not our home and it is not our resting place. There is coming a day, closer today than it has ever been, when Christ will return for His children. When He comes, we will enter into our eternal rest. Until that day, we must allow our hope to motivate us to serve with vigor and faithfulness.

I like where Paul is taking us in his prayer of thanks. Listen to what he says in verse 5. "...for our gospel did not come to you in word only, but also in power and in the Holy Spirit and with full conviction; just as you know what kind of men we proved to be among you for your sake."

The Gospel came to them in power! The Greek word here is *dunamis*, it is where we derive our word, dynamite. Think about that for a moment if you would. The Gospel is explosive, it is powerful, and it is life-transforming. Apparently, when the believers in Thessalonica heard the message of Paul and his associates, it had a powerful effect on them.

I can say this much from my own experience, and from the countless stories that I have heard from others, whenever the Bible is preached, heard, and then obeyed, lives are changed! Christianity is more than a collection of interesting facts, it is the power of God unto salvation to everyone who believes. I find it hard to spend time in God's Word and not be different when I close my Bible. When I attend worship service, and preach the word or hear the word preached, I am a different person because of it.

I do hear the opposite on more occasions than I would like. People tell me that they are not being fed at church, or that the sermon did nothing for them. They blame the pastor or evangelist for not doing their job. Let me be clear on this, it is not the pastor's job to move you, it is your job to be prepared to hear the Word and then to apply the Word that you hear. If your heart is not ready to receive the Word and if you do not apply what you are being taught, of course you will think that you are not being fed. The pastor's role is to be obedient to God and deliver the message that has been laid upon his heart.

What I am trying to communicate to you is that the pastor does not change your life. The Holy Spirit changes people when they hear, believe, and receive the Gospel! In our Scripture, Paul was thanking God for their labor. He was teaching that it was the Spirit that brought about the change in their lives. The church knew this was true because Paul, Silas, and Timothy were living out what they were teaching the church.

We should all strive to be a living example of the Gospel message. People will seek to know the power of God in their life when they see you living out the power of God in your own life. People will desire to spend more time with God in prayer when they hear and see the testimony of answered prayer in your life. The church is in desperate need of leaders and members who live out what they say they believe. The Kingdom of God is in desperate need of Christians who will be genuine in their faith and allow that faith to guide them in every aspect of their lives. God was doing great things in this church because the people were drawn to what God was doing in the life of the church.

The people at Thessalonica not only witnessed what God was doing in the life of Paul, Silas, and Timothy, they followed their example.

> You also became imitators of us and of the Lord, having received the word in much tribulation with the joy of the Holy Spirit. (verse 6 of 1 Thess. 1:2–7)

The church became imitators of these men of God. In so doing, they became imitators of the Lord. They were persecuted, but received it with joy of the Holy Spirit. How was this possible? The power of the Gospel. They had been wonderfully changed and now saw being persecuted as a privilege. They were chosen to suffer as Christ had suffered, and Paul thanked God on their behalf because of the difference this made in their lives.

Follow the progression. Paul, Silas, and Timothy were living examples of the power of the Gospel. The believers at Thessalonica saw their example, believed, and lived out this example. The result was this church became an example of the power of the Gospel to believers all over Macedonia! Talk about multiplication! This is why the church grew. They were following the pattern originally designed by Jesus to share the Gospel—baptize believers and make disciples. Herein lays the underlying secret to church growth. If you are living out what you believe, and people see you are genuine, your faith will multiply through others. Could it be that the reason many churches are not growing is because they do not see believers living out the power of the Gospel?

For the remainder of this chapter I would like us to return to verse 4 of 1 Thess. 1:2–7, and consider the implications of what Paul is teaching when he says, "knowing, brethren beloved by God, His choice of you."

The choosing of God has to do with election, and there are three specific areas of election or choosing that are important for our discussion on prayer and discovering God's power in your life.

God's election or choosing is always:

Sovereign

God freely chooses to provide salvation to whomever He wills, and we know that it is God's will for all to be saved. We also understand that not all will accept His gift of eternal life. The salvation that God provides to each of us is according to His goodness and mercy. There is nothing we can do to earn His salvation because we are not saved by our own merit.

> ...for though the twins were not yet born and had not done anything good or bad, so that God's purpose according to His choice would stand, not because of works but because of Him who calls. (Rom. 9:11)

Pretemporal

As stated above, we are not received into the family of God because we deserve it. We are received into God's family simply because of the mercy of God. He has forgiven us and saved us according to His plan, which has been established since before the foundation of the universe. I know that this thought causes many problems and brings up the argument of "free will." All we can conclude is that God's ways are higher than our ways and His thoughts are higher than our thoughts. If God works by free will, great. If God predetermines who is saved and who is not, great. Neither accepted view excuses us from our need to live and pass on the power of the Gospel message because as mere men, we do not know who is destined to receive and who is not.

> ...just as He chose us in Him before the foundation of the world, that we would be holy and blameless before Him, in love. (Eph. 1:4)

For Salvation

Our salvation begins and ends with God. We are chosen to simply accept His gift. Again, you were chosen from the beginning for salvation through sanctification. The process of sanctification is ongoing and is the process of Christian growth through which the Holy Spirit makes you more like Christ in your attitude and actions. This is good news for you and me. If we learn and accept that salvation begins and ends with God, we can be confident in whatever situation we are facing, knowing that God is in control and that He will finish in us that which He began (Phil. 1:6).

> But we should always give thanks to God for you, brethren beloved by the Lord, because God has chosen you from the beginning for salvation through sanctification by the Spirit and faith in the truth. (2 Thess. 2:13)

Your election or choosing is sovereign, pretemporal, and for salvation. Here is the thing; your election will be proven by the fruit that accompanies salvation.

> So, as those who have been chosen of God, holy
> and beloved, put on a heart of compassion,
> kindness, humility, gentleness, and patience.
> (Col. 3:12)

There is no way around it. If you have experienced the dynamic power of the Gospel, your life will be different and others will be able to see it. This is exactly what happened to those in Thessalonica.

Have you experienced the life-changing power of the Gospel of Jesus Christ? Are you living it out on a daily basis? If so, people should be able to sense the change that has taken place in your life, and that change should be positively affecting them. As a result, their lives will be having a positive affect on others as well.

We need to pray that we will hear, receive, and apply the Word of God that is taught to us weekly and that we study daily. We need to pray that the Holy Spirit will use that Word to change us into the man or woman that God intends for us to be. Finally, we need to pray that our life will be the life-changing influence that others need to see to spark their relationship with God to be what it ought to be.

Through understanding the prayers of the Apostle Paul, and praying towards these same characteristics to be found in our life, we will discover and experience the reality of the power of God in our life on a daily basis. When you experience that power it is life-changing and will impact everything you do for the Kingdom for the rest of your life.

STUDY QUESTIONS

Chapter 1

When does the indwelling of the Holy Spirit take place, and how does this affect your prayer life?

According to the text, what is the will of God?

What are the two most effective ways for releasing the power and presence of God in our lives?

Chapter 2

Even though Paul followed a pattern when he prayed, what stands out as significant to his prayers?

Even when addressing serious problems within the church, what is one thing Paul always found the opportunity to do?

What is the difference between a "Kingdom prayer" and a "Calling prayer"?

Chapter 3

How should we see "other" churches in our community?

What is one major reason why the prayer life and ministry of Paul was so successful?

What are the three results that happen when the power of God is released upon our lives?

Chapter 4

What is "grace"?

What is the importance of having the call of God in your life confirmed?

Are you currently living out the calling that God has placed upon your life?

Chapter 5

What does it mean to pray for the "riches of God" in your life?

Can your calling be affirmed even in the midst of difficulties? How?

Are you allowing the words and encouraging spirit of Christ to flow through you into the lives of others?

Chapter 6

What is significant about the spiritual gift of faith?

Why is it important for us to seek out the "greater gifts"?

What is the purpose of the gifts God has given to you and to others in your church?

Chapter 7

What trait did both Paul and John stress as authentic proof of the Gospel?

What happened to the church at Ephesus during the second generation of believers?

What are the advantages and disadvantages of enthusiasm and knowledge?

Chapter 8

How do the heresies faced by the church at Colossae compare to the heresies the church faces today?

What happens to people when they believe the Gospel message?

Have you personally committed your heart and life to Jesus Christ? Is He both your Savior and Lord?

Chapter 9

What is a natural response for those who have been forgiven by God?

Are there any implications for you and me of living out what we believe? What are some?

Your election by God is three-fold. Describe each aspect.

LaVergne, TN USA
04 February 2010
172062LV00005B/10/P